Chihuahuas

Katie Gillespie

www.openlightbox.com

Step 1
Go to **www.openlightbox.com**

Step 2
Enter this unique code
GNIZLJ75T

Step 3
Explore your interactive eBook!

AV2 is optimized for use on any device

Your interactive eBook comes with...

Contents
Browse a live contents page to easily navigate through resources

Audio
Listen to sections of the book read aloud

Videos
Watch informative video clips

Weblinks
Gain additional information for research

Slideshows
View images and captions

Try This!
Complete activities and hands-on experiments

Key Words
Study vocabulary, and complete a matching word activity

Quizzes
Test your knowledge

Share
Share titles within your Learning Management System (LMS) or Library Circulation System

Citation
Create bibliographical references following APA, CMOS, and MLA styles

ISBN 978-1-7911-3320-7

The digital components of this book are guaranteed to stay active for at least five years from the date of publication.

Chihuahuas

Contents

Name That Dog

Which dog is the world's smallest breed?

Which dog is said to have a sassy attitude?

Which dog has an apple-shaped head?

Which dog came from Mexico?

If you guessed the Chihuahua...

You are right

Chihuahua History

Although the Chihuahua's exact origin is unclear, experts believe that it is one of the oldest dog **breeds** from the Americas. The history of this tiny dog dates back hundreds of years. During the 9th century, a small, light dog breed called the Techichi was popular with the Toltec people of Mexico. These dogs are thought to be early **ancestors** of the Chihuahua.

By the 12th century, the Toltecs had been **conquered** by another group, the Aztecs. These people **bred** the Techichi to be even smaller and lighter. Over time, these small dogs spread to remote villages across Mexico. In the mid-19th century, people from the United States gave the breed the name of the Mexican state of Chihuahua after finding many of these dogs there.

Mexico is a North American country. It is bordered by the United States to the north, as well as Guatemala and Belize to the southeast.
United States
Gulf of Mexico
Mexico
Pacific Ocean
Cuba
Belize
Jamaica
Honduras
Guatemala
El Salvador
Nicaragua
Costa Rica
Panama
Colombia

The American Kennel Club (AKC) is an organization that registers dog breeds. It recognized Chihuahuas as a breed in 1904. The first individual Chihuahua registered by the AKC was recorded four years later, in 1908. His name was Beppie.

The AKC divides dog breeds into seven different groups. Dogs in each group share common traits with each other. The AKC classifies Chihuahuas as part of the Toy category. Members of this group are small, protective, and attentive. They make especially good lap dogs. Other well-known Toy breeds are the Shih Tzu, Pomeranian, and pug.

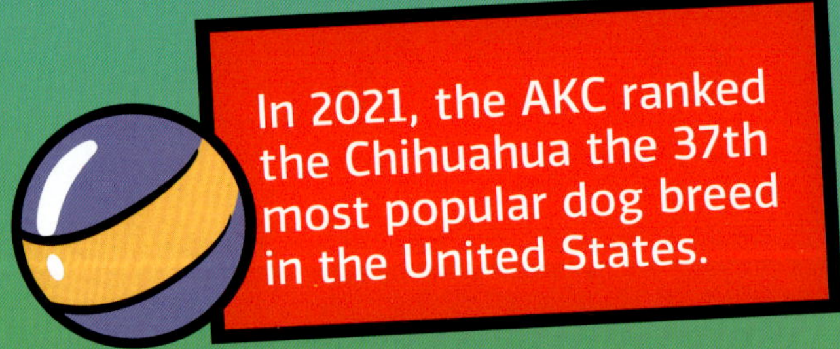

The United Kennel Club (UKC), another U.S. organization, has eight dog breed classifications. It places the Chihuahua in its Companion Group. Breeds from this category have adapted to life as family companions. This group includes breeds such as the poodle, Maltese, and Dalmatian.

A typical adult Chihuahua's weight is less than 6 pounds (2.7 kilograms).

What They Look Like

Chihuahuas are most easily recognized by their extremely small size. They stand only 5 to 8 inches (13 to 20 centimeters) high at the shoulder. Male and female Chihuahuas are typically similar in both height and weight.

These compact dogs have large ears for their size that stand up when alert. Their pointed muzzles are short, with lean cheeks and jaws. Chihuahuas have slightly arched necks and graceful shoulders.

Chihuahuas come in one of two **coat** varieties. Their coats are either long or smooth. A Chihuahua's coat should be soft in texture, with a ruff on the neck, and a full, furry tail.

Chihuahua nose and eye colors depend on the color of the dog's coat. Many Chihuahuas have noses that match their coat, although some blond dogs have pink noses. A Chihuahua's round, **luminous** eyes are often dark or ruby-colored. White or blond Chihuahuas may have light eyes.

Chihuahuas are fast-moving animals, with dainty feet. They have strong, muscular legs. A Chihuahua's tail can be positioned in one of two ways. It may be curled in a loop over the back, or held, sickle-like, away from the body.

According to the AKC, Chihuahuas can be any color, either solid or mixed.

The Chihuahua Personality

Despite their small size, Chihuahuas have big personalities. These spirited dogs make affectionate companions for the right people. They are alert, playful, and can adapt to many situations. Chihuahuas are typically loyal to their owners. Like any pet, it is important for them to be kept safe. Chihuahuas must live in a suitable environment.

Chihuahuas make ideal pets for city dwellers. They can live happily even in small homes, such as apartments.

As they get along well with each other, but not as well with other dogs, Chihuahuas do best around other Chihuahuas.

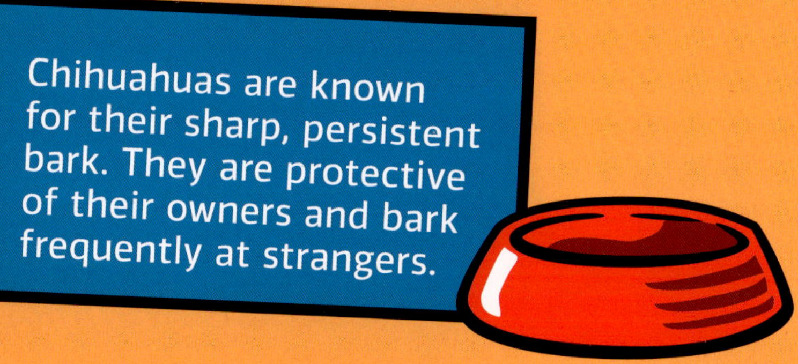

Chihuahuas are not recommended for families with young children. Children can be too rowdy for such tiny creatures. There is a risk that the dogs might accidentally be hurt while playing or roughhousing.

Households with multiple pets can be dangerous for these dogs as well. Most Chihuahuas do not realize how small they are, and often have a "big dog" attitude. Their independence and self-confidence can get them into trouble. Chihuahuas are defenseless against large dogs or other animals.

If Chihuahuas are around children or other pets, they must be closely supervised by a responsible adult. Chihuahuas should never be left alone outside. While outdoors, Chihuahuas must be leashed at all times. This stops them from running away, and allows owners to pull them away from harm, if needed.

Chihuahua Puppies

Several things determine the number of puppies in a dog's **litter**. One of these is the breed's body size. Generally, big dog breeds have more puppies than little breeds. Due to their small size, Chihuahuas have an average litter size of only one to three puppies.

Chihuahuas are born with their eyes closed, and do not open them until they are about two weeks old. These small dogs grow quickly, reaching their adult size after about nine months.

A newborn Chihuahua may weigh as little as 2.5 ounces (71 grams).

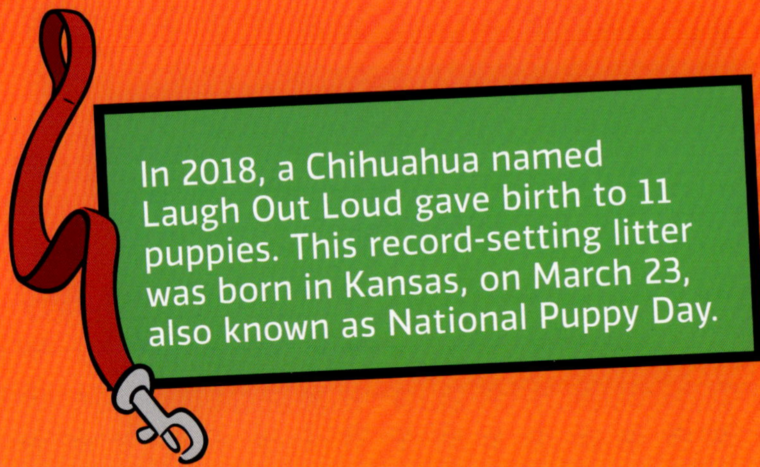

Dogs should be fed a diet that is suited for their age. Chihuahua puppies can easily become overweight. Owners must make sure they get the right amount of **calories** and **nutrients**. High-fat foods and cooked bones should be avoided.

Chihuahuas are very clever. They know that begging can help them get what they want. It is necessary for owners to establish boundaries early on, when the dogs are young. Puppies must know who is in charge. This will help them learn to behave properly as adults. Formal training can also help Chihuahua puppies grow into well-behaved adults.

Chihuahuas are born with floppy ears. These will often stand upright by the time the dog is 6 months old.

Chihuahuas may choose a single person to be their favorite companion. In a home with several owners, each should care for and play with the dog in order to make sure it bonds with all of them.

Hard at Work

Unlike many other dog breeds, Chihuahuas were not bred as working animals. Since the days of the Toltecs, these dogs have mostly served as companions. This continues to be their most popular role today. Chihuahuas form strong bonds with their owners and are very affectionate toward them.

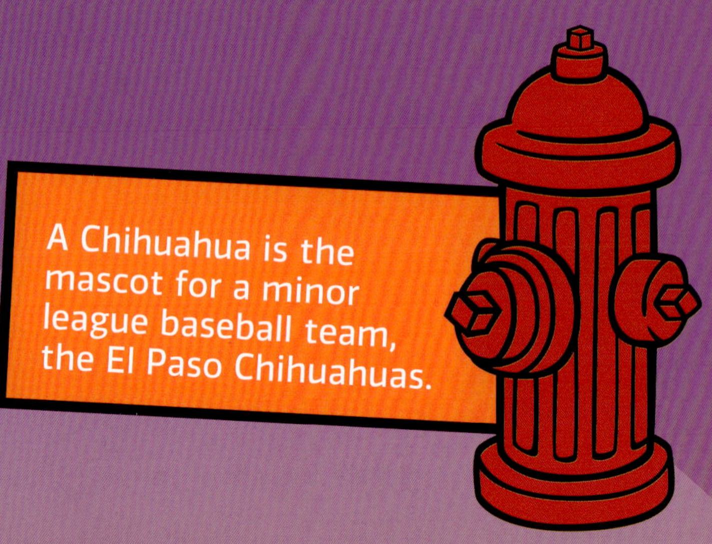

Chihuahuas are too small to defend property or act as guard dogs. However, they are considered by many to make excellent watchdogs. As Chihuahuas are very aware of their surroundings, they can bark to alert their owners to intruders or any other unusual activity.

Today, some Chihuahuas are used to control pests. In rural parts of Mexico, they are often used as "ratters." Their natural instincts and bravery make them ideal for catching rats, squirrels, and other small rodents.

Other Chihuahuas work as performers. They may take part in dog shows. Some Chihuahuas have also appeared in movies, television shows, and commercials.

A Chihuahua's strong sense of hearing means it can often notice strangers before its owners do.

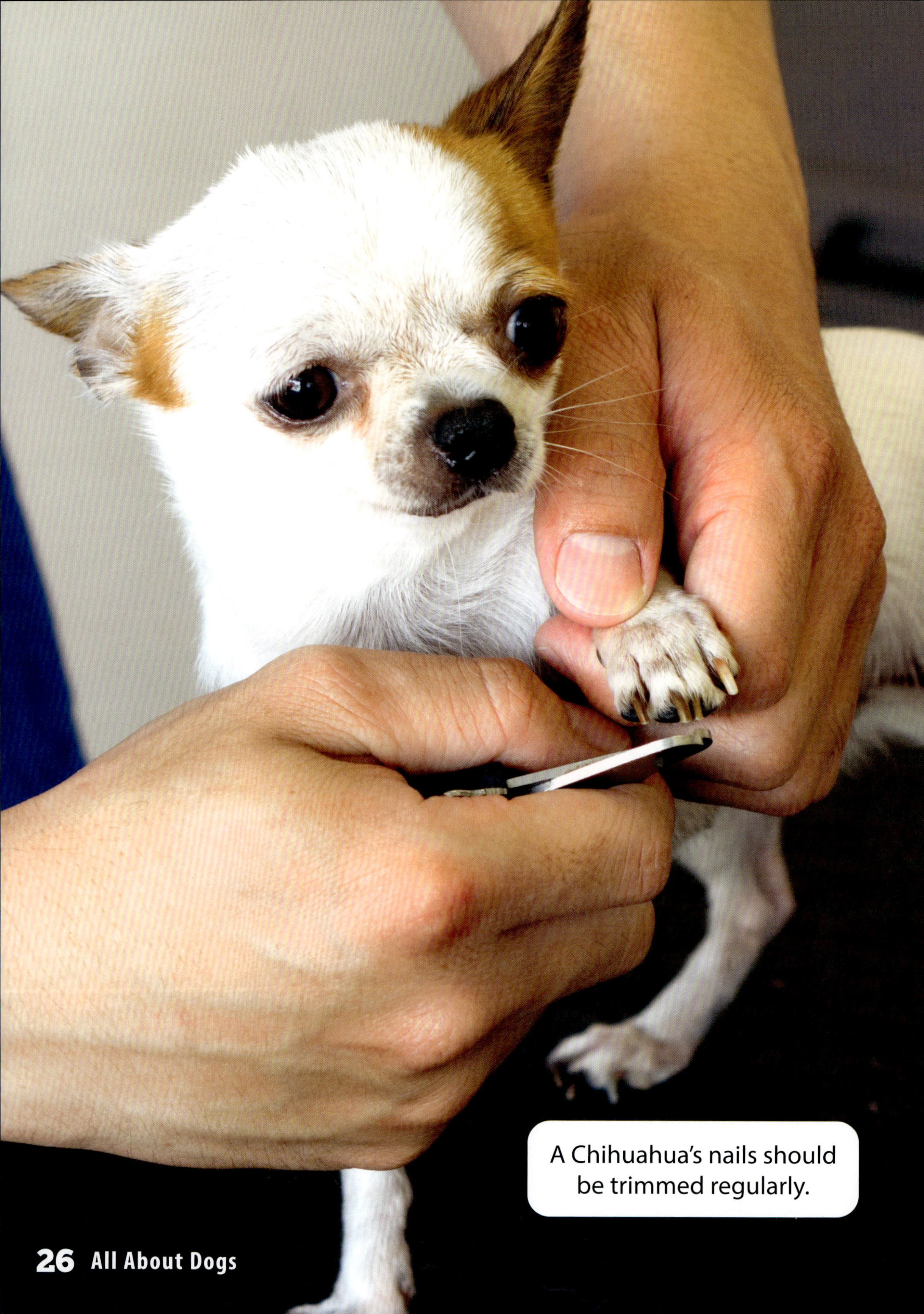

A Chihuahua's nails should be trimmed regularly.

Caring for a Chihuahua

Many Chihuahuas are quite energetic. However, as they are so small, they can usually get enough exercise simply by following their owners around the house. If a Chihuahua is taken for a walk, the trip should be kept slow and short.

Chihuahuas do not **shed** very much. Their grooming needs depend on the type of coat they have. Long-haired Chihuahuas may require brushing more than once per week to keep their coats from getting tangled. Chihuahuas with smooth coats often only need to be brushed occasionally. Regardless of coat, a Chihuahua should have regular baths, and its ears should be checked and cleaned when necessary.

A Chihuahua's teeth should be brushed regularly. Special dental treats may also be given, as recommended by a veterinarian.

Chihuahuas are a generally healthy breed. However, they do have certain health issues. The most common of these include **dislocated** kneecaps, eye problems, and heart disease. Experts suggest that Chihuahuas should undergo regular exams from **veterinarians** to check for these issues.

Caring for a pet requires a great deal of patience and hard work. It is also a big financial and time commitment. Compared to other dog breeds, Chihuahuas live particularly long lives. They have a life expectancy of 14 to 16 years. Before choosing a Chihuahua, owners must be sure they are ready to take on such a large responsibility. Those who do will be rewarded with a lifetime of love and companionship.

Special attention must be paid to Chihuahuas in cold climates. These dogs get cold very easily, causing them to shiver. Some owners dress their Chihuahuas in sweaters to help keep them warm.

Chihuahua Quiz

Q: What two coat varieties can a Chihuahua have?

A: Long or smooth

Q: How much does a Chihuahua weigh?

A: No more than 6 pounds (2.7 kg)

Q: Where are Chihuahuas often employed as "ratters"?

A: In rural parts of Mexico

Q: What breed was an early ancestor of the Chihuahua?

A: The Techichi

Q: How many puppies are in an average Chihuahua litter?

A: One to three

Q: How long is a Chihuahua's life expectancy?

A: 14 to 16 years

Key Words

ancestors (AN-seh-strz): people or animals in the same family who lived in the past

bred (BRED): produced offspring

breeds (BREEDZ): certain types of animals

calories (KA-lr-eez): energy from food

coat (KOHT): a dog's fur

conquered (KAANG-krd): overcome by force

dislocated (DIS-low-kay-tuhd): put out of something's proper place

litter (LI-tr): a group of babies born to one animal at the same time

luminous (LOO-muh-nuhs): shining

nutrients (NOO-tree-uhnts): parts of food that help things live and grow

shed (SHED): when fur naturally falls off

veterinarians (veh-truh-NEH-ree-uhns): doctors who take care of animals

Index

Get the best of both worlds.

AV2 bridges the gap between print and digital.

The expandable resources toolbar enables quick access to content including **videos**, **audio**, **activities**, **weblinks**, **slideshows**, **quizzes**, and **key words**.

Animated videos make static images come alive.

Resource icons on each page help readers to further **explore key concepts**.

Published by Lightbox Learning Inc.
276 5th Avenue, Suite 704 #917
New York, NY 10001
Website: www.openlightbox.com

Library of Congress Control Number: 2023008471

ISBN 978-1-7911-5639-8 (hardcover)
ISBN 978-1-7911-5640-4 (softcover)
ISBN 978-1-7911-5641-1 (multi-user eBook)

Printed in Guangzhou, China
1 2 3 4 5 6 7 8 9 0 27 26 25 24 23

042023
101322

Project Coordinator: John Willis
Designer: Terry Paulhus

Photo Credits
Every reasonable effort has been made to trace ownership and to obtain permission to reprint copyright material. The publisher would be pleased to have any errors or omissions brought to its attention so that they may be corrected in subsequent printings. The publisher acknowledges Alamy, Minden Pictures, Newscom, Shutterstock, and Wikimedia as its primary image suppliers for this title.